SWEAR WORD COLORING BOOK

Hilarious (and Disturbing) Adult Coloring Books

Free Stuff?
Yes Please!

Like free stuff? So do we! Come check out the site and get yourself some freebies!

www.swearwordcoloringbooks.com/bonus

I take great pride in my art, but even more pride expanding your dictionary into new lands of depravity. However, please keep these new words from children....they are our future for fucks sake!!! This book may not be for kids, but it'll certainly tug at your inner child. Coloring puts a big smile on my face, but coloring the word assbag makes me laugh out loud. I hope you will too.

Now Sit the F*ck Down and Color.

Bullshit

DUMBSHIT

Limpdick

Jackass

BITCH

Cocksucker

buttlicker

Goddamn

FUCKSTICK

SUMTART

ASSBAG

BASTARD

Fatass

Queef

Motherfucker

BUTTFACE

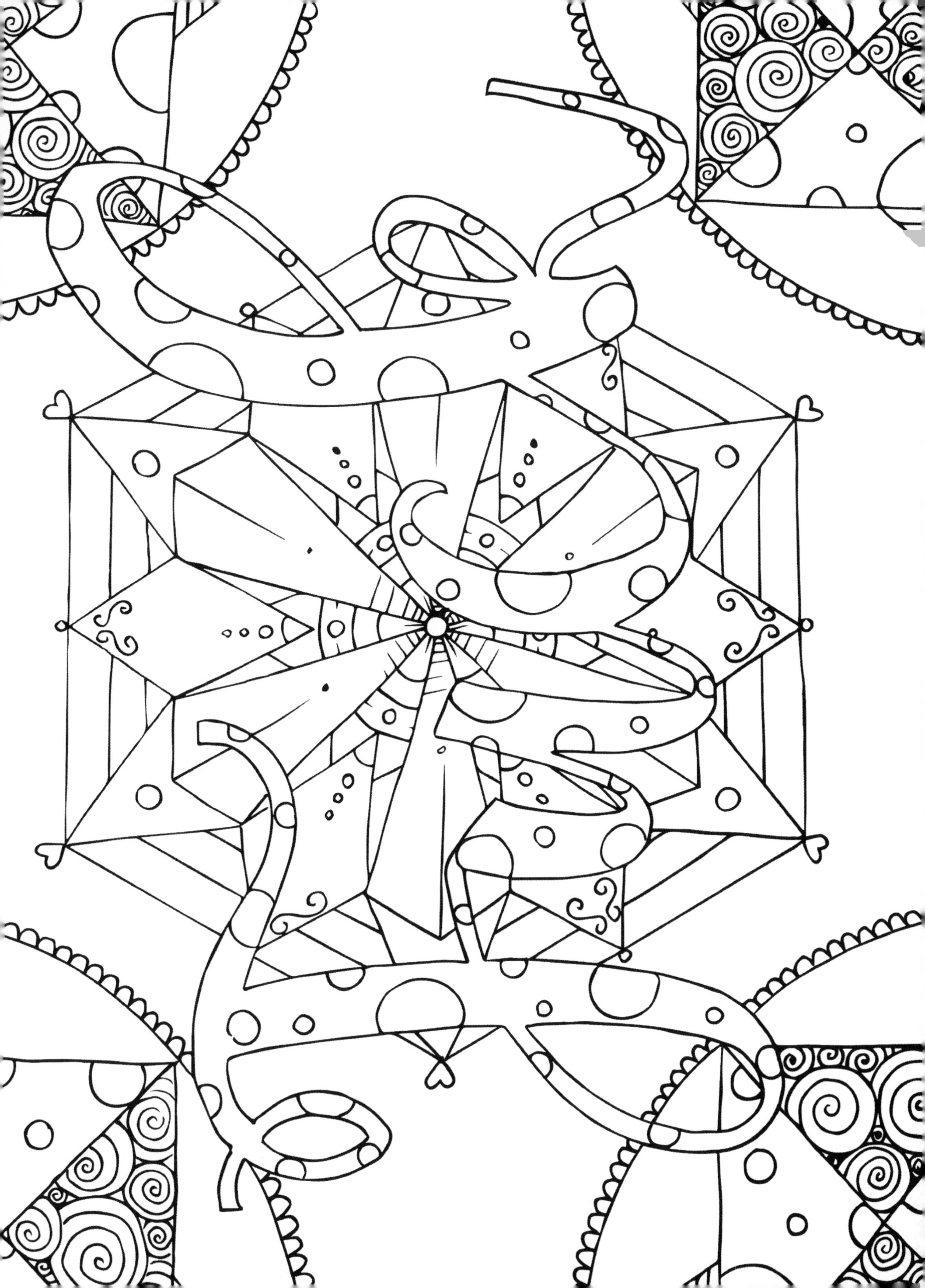

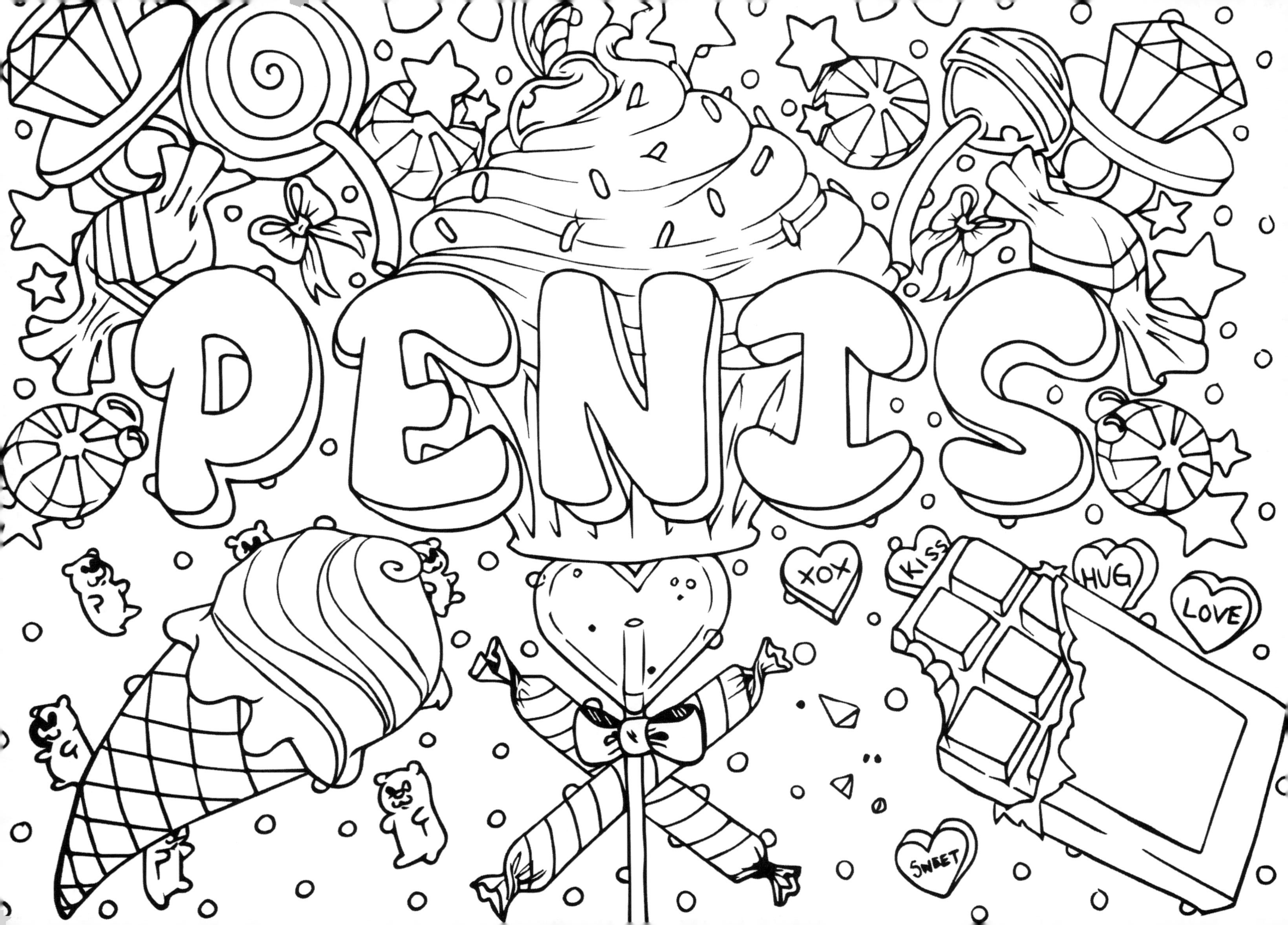
PENIS
XOX
KISS
HUG
LOVE
SWEET